WEEKLY WORD SORTS THAT BUILD SPELLING SKILLS

Easy Week-by-Week Reproducibles and Activities That Teach Kids
the Key Spelling Rules and Patterns They Need to Become Effective Spellers

by Kristina Arcuri Maher

NEW YORK • TORONTO • LONDON • AUCKLAND • SYDNEY
MEXICO CITY • NEW DELHI • HONG KONG • BUENOS AIRES

SCHOLASTIC
Teaching
Resources

This book is dedicated to my family:
My husband, Dan
My parents, Kathy and Tony
My sister, Audrey

Thank you for your constant love, encouragement, and support!

Special thanks to my friends at the Waugh School District
for creating such a wonderful place for children and such a great place to work!

Cover design by Maria Lilja
Cover illustration by Rick Brown
Interior design by Solutions by Design, Inc.

ISBN: 0-439-21615-X

Copyright © 2003 by Kristina Arcuri Maher.
Published by Scholastic Inc.
Printed in the U.S.A.

5 6 7 8 9 10   40   10 09 08 07 06 05

CONTENTS

INTRODUCTION

Welcome to *Weekly Word Sorts That Build Spelling Skills*—an easy-to-manage program that helps students become more effective spellers through weekly hands-on activities. Each week, students receive a set of spelling word cards and a sorting sheet. They study the words, find similarities and differences, and sort the word cards into categories. The process of manipulating word cards, making predictions, and drawing conclusions about words helps students remember and apply spelling concepts on tests and in their writing.

Each of the activities in this book reinforces a key spelling pattern or rule. Once students understand the pattern or rule, they can spell dozens of similar words. You'll find activities that focus on the topics second and third graders need the most practice with—plurals, silent letter patterns, verbs, homophones, contractions, and more.

How to Use This Book

This program includes 36 word-sorting activities, one for every week of the school year. The activities are organized into five parts: Vowels; Blends and Digraphs; Consonant Sounds and Silent Letter Patterns; Plurals, Word Endings, Verbs, and Suffixes; and Word Study (homophones, contractions, and more). You might use the activities in the order they are presented, or you might move from section to section based on the needs of your students and the requirements of your curriculum. After choosing the week's activity, read through the teaching ideas that go along with it (pages 6–23). For each activity, you'll find:

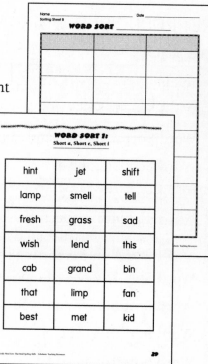

SORTING ACTIVITIES
The first sorting activity listed reinforces the main rule or spelling patterns. Subsequent activities challenge students to sort by parts of speech, number of letters or syllables, and so on, to give students additional practice with the words.

WORD LIST
Each word list shows the words grouped into categories specified in the first sorting activity. The same words appear on the reproducible word cards.

SPELLING JOURNAL
This section provides two to three quick activities that students can complete in an ongoing journal. Activities challenge students to explain their sorting rationales, make lists of additional words, use the week's spelling words in creative writing assignments, and more. At the beginning of the year, give each student a spiral notebook or other journal in which they can complete these assignments.

REPRODUCIBLE WORD CARDS
Each activity comes with a set of word cards (pages 29–64). The 20-card sets can be sorted into two categories on Sorting Sheet A, and the 21-card sets can be sorted into three categories on Sorting Sheet B.

WEEKLY SPELLING PLAN

This daily plan provides one way to incorporate spelling practice into your teaching each day. Feel free to adapt this plan as you see fit.

DAY 1:

Introduce the spelling rule or pattern to students and present or brainstorm together words that follow this rule or pattern. Write these words on chart paper or an overhead transparency. Discuss the patterns of the words and ask students how they might sort them.

DAY 2:

Give each student a copy of the word cards and the appropriate sorting sheet. For quick reference, have them fill in the number of the word sort on the blank line at the top. Then show students where to write the sorting categories at the top of each column on the sorting sheet. You might provide students with the categories or challenge them to discover them on their own. Have students cut apart their cards and sort them on the sorting sheet. If students will use the cards for additional sorting activities, they can store the cards in small resealable plastic bags. If you would like to collect the sorting sheets for assessment, instruct students either to write or glue the words on the sorting sheet.

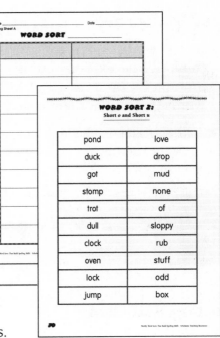

DAY 3:

Assign students one or more of the spelling journal activities. This can be completed during class or as homework.

DAY 4:

Have students sort the words in another way or complete another spelling journal activity. When completing additional sorting activities, students can simply group together cards on their desks rather than using a sorting sheet. For a greater challenge, have students work together to think of additional words that follow the week's spelling pattern or rule. They can search for words around the classroom and in books or magazines. Students can then create cards for these words and sort them into categories.

DAY 5:

For assessment, give students a chance to show what they know on a quiz. Include both the words from the week and a general question about the spelling pattern or rule. You might use their spelling journal assignments as a part of the assessment.

WORD SORT 1:
Short *a*, Short *e*, Short *i*

Sorting Activities

- Give each student a copy of the word cards (page 29) and Sorting Sheet B (page 28) to sort by words with short-*a*, short-*e*, and short-*i* sounds. (Answers appear at right.)

- Sort by number of letters.

Spelling Journal

- All the words end in consonants. Why do you think this is? Explain your reasons with examples. (Words that end with a vowel, such as words that end in silent *e*, usually have a long middle vowel.)

- Add words to each category.

Short *a*	Short *e*	Short *i*
cab	best	bin
fan	fresh	hint
grand	jet	kid
grass	lend	limp
lamp	met	shift
sad	smell	this
that	tell	wish

WORD SORT 2:
Short *o* and Short *u*

Sorting Activities

- Give each student a copy of the word cards (page 30) and Sorting Sheet A (page 27) to sort by short-*o* and short-*u* sounds. (Answers appear at right.)

- Sort the short-*u* words into two categories: words that have a *u* in them and words that don't.

Spelling Journal

- Did you place any words in the short-*u* column that do not have the letter *u* in them? Why or why not?

- What other words do you know that fit these patterns? List them in two columns.

Short *o*	Short *u*
box	duck
clock	dull
drop	jump
got	love
lock	mud
odd	none
pond	of
sloppy	oven
stomp	rub
trot	stuff

WORD SORT 3:
Long *a*

Sorting Activities

- Give each student a copy of the word cards (page 31) and Sorting Sheet A (page 27) to sort by long-*a* spelling patterns of *a_e* and *ai*. (Answers appear at right.)

- Sort by words that include a blend or digraph and words that do not.

- Sort by number of letters.

Spelling Journal

- Can you think of any other long-*a* spelling patterns? (*ay, eak, eigh*) Make a list of words that include these patterns.

- Which of the words are homophones? List the homophone pairs. (*plane, plain; pain, pane; sail, sale; wait, weight*)

a_e	ai
bake	braid
brave	chain
face	claim
fade	nail
late	pain
maze	raid
name	sail
plane	snail
rage	vain
scale	wait

WORD SORT 4:
Long *e*

Sorting Activities

- Give each student a copy of the word cards (page 32) and Sorting Sheet B (page 28) to sort words by long-*e* spelling patterns of *ea*, *ee*, and *ie*. (Answers appear at right.)

- Sort words by number of letters.

- Sort words into two categories: those that end with a vowel and those that end with a consonant.

ea	ee	ie
feast	cheek	brief
grease	feed	chief
leave	heel	grief
meal	peek	niece
peach	screen	piece
scream	squeeze	shield
tea	steep	yield

Spelling Journal

- Can you think of another long-*e* spelling pattern? (*e: be, he, me*) Make a list of words that include this pattern.

- Which words are difficult for you to remember? Can you think of any ways to remember how to spell them?

WORD SORT 5:
Long *i*

Sorting Activities

- Give each student a copy of the word cards (page 33) and Sorting Sheet A (page 27) to sort by the long-*i* patterns of *i_e* and *igh*. (Answers appear at right.)

- Sort the *igh* words into two categories: words that end in *igh* and words that end in *ight*.

Spelling Journal

- What other words include these spelling patterns? Write them in two columns.

- What other spelling patterns can you think of for long *i*? Write several words for each of these patterns. (*ie, ild, ind*).

- Can you think of any spelling patterns for long *i* that do not include the letter *i*? (*uy, y, ye*)

i_e	igh
alive	delight
bike	fight
dime	high
divide	might
hive	sigh
mile	sight
mine	sunlight
polite	thigh
time	tight
wise	tonight

WORD SORT 6:
Long *o*

Sorting Activities

- Give each student a copy of the word cards (page 34) and Sorting Sheet B (page 28) to sort by the patterns of *ow*, *oa*, and *o_e*. (Answers appear at right.)

- Sort by words that end with a consonant and words that end with a vowel.

Spelling Journal

- Explain how you sorted these words.

- What other words include these spelling patterns? Write them in three columns.

- Can you think of other spelling patterns for long *o*? (*oe, oll, olt, ost*, and *old*) Write a few words for each long-*o* spelling pattern.

ow	oa	o_e
elbow	boat	code
flow	coal	globe
follow	float	joke
glow	roam	rope
grow	soak	spoke
known	soap	stove
window	toast	vote

WORD SORT 7:
/o͝o/ and /o͞o/

Sorting Activities

- Give each student a copy of the word cards (page 35) and Sorting Sheet A (page 27) to sort by the sounds of /o͝o/ and /o͞o/. (Answers appear at right.) Have them read the words aloud quietly in order to hear the differences in pronunciation.

- Sort into groups of words that rhyme.

Spelling Journal

- Can words be spelled differently but have the same sound? Provide some examples.

- Were some words hard to sort? Which ones, and why?

- List words that fit into each category.

/o͝o/	/o͞o/
brook	boots
cook	broom
good	hoop
hook	moose
look	mood
shook	noon
should	roof
stood	school
took	shoot
would	tool

WORD SORT 8:
/o͞o/ and /yo͞o/

Sorting Activities

- Give each student a copy of the word cards (page 36) and Sorting Sheet A (page 27) to sort by the sounds of /o͞o/ and /yo͞o/. (Answers appear at right.) Have students quietly read the words aloud in order to hear the differences in pronunciation.

- Sort by words that end with a consonant and words that end with a vowel.

- Sort the words with /o͞o/ by the spelling patterns *ue*, *ew*, and *u_e*.

Spelling Journal

- Were some words hard to sort? Which ones, and why? Can you think of ways to help you remember how to spell them?

- Add words to each category. They might have the same spelling patterns or different ones.

/o͞o/	/yo͞o/
blue	amuse
booth	cube
chew	cute
clue	fuse
drew	human
glue	menu
June	mule
rude	music
rule	unit
tune	use

WORD SORT 9:
ou and *ow*

Sorting Activities

- Give each student a copy of the word cards (page 37) and Sorting Sheet A (page 27) to sort by words with *ou* and words with *ow*. (Answers appear at right.)
- Sort by number of letters.

Spelling Journal

- List the words that rhyme and then write a short poem using these words.
- Write an advertisement for any product. Use as many words from the list as you can in your ad.

ou	*ow*
bounce	allow
cloudy	down
count	frown
hour	growl
loud	howl
mouth	owl
our	plow
out	powder
round	town
south	wow

WORD SORT 10:
au and *aw*

Sorting Activities

- Give each student a copy of the word cards (page 38) and Sorting Sheet A (page 27) to sort by words with *au* or *aw*. (Answers appear at right.)
- Sort the words in alphabetical order.

Spelling Journal

- Add words to each category.
- Write a letter to a friend using words from the list and other words with *au* or *aw*.
- Make a word search using words from the list.

au	*aw*
August	awful
author	claw
because	dawn
caught	draw
cause	flaw
daughter	jaw
fault	lawn
haul	paw
pause	seesaw
taught	yawn

WORD SORT 11:
i before e

Sorting Activities

• Give each student a copy of the word cards (page 39) and Sorting Sheet A (page 27). Teach the rule "*i before e* except after *c* or when sounding like an *a* as in *neighbor* or *sleigh*." Have students sort by words with *i before e* and words with *e before i*. (Answers appear at right.)

• Sort by words that end with a vowel and words that end with a consonant.

Spelling Journal

• Can you think of words that do not follow this rule? (*either, foreign, height, leisure, neither, science, weird*, and so on)

• Draw a comic strip that teaches the "*i before e*" rule.

i before e	*e before i*
believe	ceiling
chief	eight
field	neighbor
fierce	receipt
friend	receive
friendly	reign
niece	reindeer
piece	sleigh
relief	vein
thief	weigh

WORD SORT 12:
Blends *br, gr, tr*

Sorting Activities

• Give each student a copy of the word cards (page 40) and Sorting Sheet B (page 28) to sort by words with *br, gr,* and *tr*. (Answers appear at right.)

• Sort words by their part of speech. Group together nouns, adjectives, and verbs. (There is one adverb.)

Spelling Journal

• What other blends can you think of with the letter *r* in them? (*cr, dr, fr, pr*) Write words that include each of these blends.

• Write an advertisement for *r*-blends. Use as many words with *r*-blends in your ad as you can.

br	*gr*	*tr*
bread	grab	trace
breakfast	grade	track
breeze	grapes	travel
brick	great	treat
broken	green	tries
brother	grew	true
brown	group	truly

WORD SORT 13:
Blends *bl, cl, fl*

Sorting Activities

- Give each student a copy of the word cards (page 41) and Sorting Sheet B (page 28) to sort by words with *bl, cl, fl*. (Answers appear at right.)

- Sort words by their part of speech: nouns, adjectives, and verbs.

- Sort words with long vowels into one group and words with short vowels into another.

bl	cl	fl
blame	clap	flag
blanket	clean	flew
blend	cling	floor
blew	close	flour
blind	closet	flower
blink	clown	flute
block	club	fly

Spelling Journal

- What other blends can you think of with the letter *l* in them? (*gl, pl, sl*) Write words that include each of these blends.

- Write a journal entry that includes as many *l*-blends as you can.

WORD SORT 14:
Initial and Ending Blends *sk* and *st*

Sorting Activities

- Give each student a copy of the word cards (page 42) and Sorting Sheet A (page 27) to sort by words with *sk* or *st* at the beginning of the word and *sk* or *st* at the end of the word. (Answers appear at right.)

- Sort by words that include *st* and words that include *sk*.

- Sort by number of letters.

Initial Blends	Ending Blends
ski	ask
skill	brisk
skin	desk
skirt	mask
sky	risk
stain	fast
stairs	last
start	must
state	test
stone	west

Spelling Journal

- List other blends that begin with *s* (*sc, sm, sn, sp,* and so on). Then list words that begin with each blend.

- Write a story based on a fairy tale. Include as many *s*-blends as you can.

WORD SORT 15:
Initial and Ending Digraphs *ch* and *sh*

Sorting Activities

- Give each student a copy of the word cards (page 43) and Sorting Sheet A (page 27) to sort by words that include *ch* and words that include *sh*. (Answers appear at right.)

- Sort by words with *ch* or *sh* at the beginning of the word and at the end of the word.

Spelling Journal

- Say each word aloud. Which words do you have difficulty remembering how to spell? Can you think of any ways to remember them? Write your ideas in your journal.

- A digraph is two consonants in a row that stand for one sound. Can you think of any other digraphs? (*th, wh, ph, gh, ng*) Write words that include each digraph.

- Write additional words that begin with *sh* or *ch*. Then write words that end with *sh* or *ch*.

ch	*sh*
beach	brush
bunch	cash
church	crash
couch	fish
reach	trash
chance	sheet
cheese	shiny
chill	shirt
chop	shoe
chores	shout

WORD SORT 16:
Digraphs *wh* and *th*

Sorting Activities

- Give each student a copy of the word cards (page 44) and Sorting Sheet A (page 27) to sort by words with *wh* or *th*. (Answers appear at right.)

- Group together words that end with silent *e*.

Spelling Journal

- Which of these words can you use to begin a question? Write questions that begin with words from the list.

- Which of these words are the most difficult to remember? Write ways you can remember how to spell them.

- Add words to each category.

wh	*th*
whack	both
whale	other
what	than
wheel	their
when	then
where	thick
while	thing
whisper	think
white	thirty
why	though

WORD SORT 17:
ch and *tch*

Sorting Activities

- Give each student a copy of the word cards (page 45) and Sorting Sheet A (page 27) to sort by words with *ch* or *tch*. (Answers appear at right.)

- Sort the words in alphabetical order.

- Sort by number of letters.

Spelling Journal

- Can you think of other words that end with *ch* or *tch*? List them in your journal.

- Write a poem using *ch* words. Then write another poem using *tch* words.

ch	*tch*
bench	catch
each	crutch
inch	ditch
much	fetch
munch	itch
punch	match
reach	pitch
rich	stretch
such	watch
which	witch

WORD SORT 18:
Words With /f/

Sorting Activities

- Give each student a copy of the word cards (page 46) and Sorting Sheet B (page 28) to sort by words with *ph*, *gh*, and *f*. (Answers appear at right.)

- Sort by words with /f/ as the beginning sound, middle sound, or ending sound.

Spelling Journal

- A digraph is two consonants in a row that stand for one sound. Can you think of any other digraphs? (*th*, *wh*, *ch*, *sh*, *ng*) Write words that include each digraph.

- Write a letter to a friend using as many words from the list as you can.

ph	*gh*	*f*
elephant	cough	fifteen
graph	coughed	forever
nephew	enough	life
orphan	laugh	proof
phone	laughter	raft
photo	rough	shelf
trophy	tough	spoonful

WORD SORT 19:
Words With /k/

Sorting Activities

- Give each student a copy of the word cards (page 47) and Sorting Sheet B (page 28) to sort words with /k/ by the spelling patterns of c, k, and ck. (Answers appear at right.)

- Sort by words with /k/ as the beginning sound, middle sound, or ending sound.

Spelling Journal

- Write a short story using as many words with the /k/ sound as possible. It could be about a cool captain or a cranky cow! Try to include words with c, k, and ck.

- Add words to each category.

c	k	ck
candy	awake	bucket
captain	baked	chicken
coat	kite	locker
cold	shrink	luck
corn	thank	pocket
cover	turkey	rock
curve	work	sick

WORD SORT 20:
Words with /z/

Sorting Activities

- Give each student a copy of the word cards (page 48) and Sorting Sheet A (page 27) to sort words by the patterns of se and z. (Answers appear at right.)

- Sort by number of syllables.

Spelling Journal

- Which words are hard for you to remember? What can you do to remember how to spell them?

- Write a limerick or haiku using words with the /z/ sound. Include both spelling patterns listed at right.

se	z
cheese	dozen
choose	freeze
lose	lazily
please	organize
rise	prize
rose	quiz
tease	realize
these	size
those	zero
whose	zipper

WORD SORT 21:
kn, mb, wr

Sorting Activities

- Give each student a copy of the word cards (page 49) and Sorting Sheet B (page 28) to sort by words with the silent consonant patterns *kn*, *mb*, and *wr*. (Answers appear at right.)

- Sort by words with long and short vowels.

- Sort by number of letters.

Spelling Journal

- Look at the silent letter patterns in these words. Make up a rule about silent letters and then test it with different words to see if it is true.

- Which words are hard for you to remember? What can you do to remember how to spell them?

- Can you think of other words with silent letters? Make a list of them.

kn	mb	wr
knee	climb	wrap
knew	comb	wrench
knife	crumb	wrinkle
knight	lamb	wrist
knock	limb	write
knot	numb	wrong
know	thumb	wrote

WORD SORT 22:
dge and ge

Sorting Activities

- Give each student a copy of the word cards (page 50) and Sorting Sheet A (page 27) to sort by words with *dge* and *ge*. (Answers appear at right.)

- Sort by words with long and short vowels.

Spelling Journal

- Add words to each category.

- Write a description of a village that includes many different people, creatures, objects, or places whose names include either *ge* or *dge* (badgers, lodges, fudge shops, judges, stages, and so on).

dge	ge
badge	age
bridge	cage
budge	change
edge	huge
fudge	large
hedge	page
judge	plunge
ledge	sponge
pledge	stage
ridge	village

WORD SORT 23:
c and s

Sorting Activities

- Give each student a copy of the word cards (page 51) and Sorting Sheet A (page 27) to sort /s/ words spelled with c and /s/ words spelled with s. (Answers appear at right.)

- Sort by words that include blends or digraphs and words that don't.

Spelling Journal

- What do you notice about words with /s/ that are spelled with a c? Is there a pattern? (The letter c comes before e or i.)

- Alliteration is when writers use the same sound several times in a row. Read aloud the previous sentence. Do you hear the alliteration? Try to write your own alliterative sentences using as many words with the /s/ sound as possible. Include words that are spelled with c and with s.

c	s
center	case
circle	frost
excite	house
fence	loose
lace	purse
office	serve
place	smile
police	soft
price	spend
rice	worse

WORD SORT 24:
Plurals

Sorting Activities

- Give each student a copy of the word cards (page 52) and Sorting Sheet B (page 28) to sort words by their plural endings. In the first column, group plural nouns that are formed by adding s. In the second column, group plural nouns that are formed by adding es. In the third column, group plural nouns that are formed by changing the y to i and then adding es. (Answers appear at right.)

- Sort words into alphabetical order.

s	es	ies
cups	beaches	babies
flakes	boxes	cities
goals	coaches	families
grades	dishes	flies
pools	inches	pennies
spoons	lunches	spies
teams	tomatoes	stories

Spelling Journal

- If you change a singular noun that is the subject of a sentence to make it plural, do you need to change the verb? Write some examples.

- Write a paragraph with as many plural nouns as you can. Include people, places, and things.

WORD SORT 25:
Unusual Plurals

Sorting Activities

- Give each student a copy of the word cards (page 53) and Sorting Sheet A (page 27) to sort by singular and plural nouns. Have students match each singular noun with its plural form and place them side by side on the sorting sheet. (Answers appear at right.)

- Sort by words with long and short vowels.

- Sort into three categories: words that name people, animals, and things.

Spelling Journal

- Write a story using as many of the plural nouns from the list as you can.

- Choose a familiar tune and write song lyrics that include the singular and plural nouns from the list.

Singular Noun	Unusual Plural Noun
child	children
deer	deer
foot	feet
goose	geese
mouse	mice
ox	oxen
person	people
sheep	sheep
tooth	teeth
woman	women

WORD SORT 26:
-le or -el

Sorting Activities

- Give each student a copy of the word cards (page 54) and Sorting Sheet A (page 27) to sort words by -le and -el. (Answers appear at right.)

- Group together the words that have a double consonant, such as riddle.

Spelling Journal

- Add words to each category.

- Can you think of words that begin with le and el? Write words that begin with each.

-le	-el
apple	bagel
bubble	cancel
cable	flannel
candle	hotel
cattle	label
middle	nickel
pebble	parcel
sprinkle	shovel
table	towel
title	vowel

WORD SORT 27:
-ed Verbs

Sorting Activities

○ Give each student a copy of the word cards (page 55) and Sorting Sheet A (page 27) to sort by verb endings: + -ed or double the final consonant + -ed. (Answers appear at right.)

○ Sort in alphabetical order.

Spelling Journal

○ What do the verbs in each column have in common? Can you find the spelling patterns for adding -ed? (The verbs in the first column were formed by adding -ed to the verb. The verbs in the second column end with a consonant following a short vowel. They were formed by doubling the final consonant before adding -ed.) Can you think of other verbs that follow each pattern? Write them in two columns.

+ -ed	Double Final Consonant + -ed
asked	clapped
climbed	grabbed
cooked	hopped
jumped	hugged
laughed	patted
learned	shopped
relaxed	slammed
sorted	stirred
tested	stopped
walked	tapped

WORD SORT 28:
-ing Verbs

Sorting Activities

○ Give each student a copy of the word cards (page 56) and Sorting Sheet A (page 27) to sort by verb endings: + -ing or double the final consonant + -ing. (Answers appear at right.)

Spelling Journal

○ What do the verbs in each column have in common? Can you find the spelling patterns for adding -ing? (The verbs in the first column were formed by adding -ing to the verb. The verbs in the second column end with a consonant following a short vowel. They were formed by doubling the final consonant before adding -ing.) Can you think of other verbs that follow each pattern? Write them in two columns.

Verb + -ing	Double Final Consonant + -ing
bringing	begging
drawing	flipping
feeling	letting
going	mopping
mixing	running
reading	sipping
singing	sitting
speaking	tipping
talking	tugging
thinking	wagging

○ Choose a few verbs from the list and write a sentence with each.

WORD SORT 29:
-ed and -ing Verbs

Sorting Activities

- Give each student a copy of the word cards (page 57) and Sorting Sheet B (page 28) to sort by verb, verb + -*ed*, and verb + -*ing*. (Answers appear at right.)
- Sort the words in alphabetical order.

Spelling Journal

- What do the words in the first column have in common? Can you find the spelling pattern that they follow when adding -*ed* or -*ing*? (They are all verbs that end with a silent *e*. Before adding -*ed* or -*ing*, drop the *e*.) Can you think of other verbs that follow this pattern? Write them in three columns: verb, verb + -*ed*, verb + -*ing*.

Verb	Verb + -*ed*	Verb + -*ing*
chase	chased	chasing
dance	danced	dancing
hope	hoped	hoping
move	moved	moving
race	raced	racing
skate	skated	skating
taste	tasted	tasting

WORD SORT 30:
y to i Verbs

Sorting Activities

- Give each student a copy of the word cards (page 58) and Sorting Sheet B (page 28) to sort by verb, verb + -*ed*, and verb + -*ing*. (Answers appear at right.)
- Sort the words alphabetically.

Spelling Journal

- What do the words in the first column have in common? Can you find the spelling pattern that they follow when adding -*ed* or -*ing*? (They are all verbs that end with a *y* following a consonant. Before adding -*ed*, change the *y* to *i*. Keep the *y* when adding -*ing*.) Can you think of other verbs that follow this pattern? Write them in three columns: verb, verb + -*ed*, verb + -*ing*.

Verb	Verb + -*ed*	Verb + -*ing*
bury	buried	burying
carry	carried	carrying
cry	cried	crying
hurry	hurried	hurrying
study	studied	studying
try	tried	trying
worry	worried	worrying

WORD SORT 31:
Suffixes -ful, -less, -ness

Sorting Activities

- Give each student a copy of the word cards (page 59) and Sorting Sheet B (page 28) to sort by *-ful, -less, -ness*. (Answers appear at right.)

- Sort the words alphabetically.

Spelling Journal

- What are the root words of the words on the list? (*bold, dark, good*, and so on). Write the root word of each. Do any of the words have the same root words?

- Which root word was changed before adding the suffix? (*happy*)

- What do you think each suffix means? Write your ideas for each, using the words on the list as examples. (The suffix *-ful* means full of; *-less* means lack of; and *-ness* means state or condition.) Can you think of other words with these suffixes? Make a list of them.

-ful	-less	-ness
careful	careless	boldness
cheerful	endless	darkness
helpful	helpless	goodness
hopeful	hopeless	happiness
joyful	nameless	hardness
skillful	sleepless	kindness
useful	useless	softness

WORD SORT 32:
Homophones

Sorting Activities

- Give each student a copy of the word cards (page 60) and Sorting Sheet A (page 27) to sort pairs of homophones. Have students place each pair of homophones side by side on the sorting sheet. (Answers appear at right.)

Spelling Journal

- A homophone is a word that is pronounced like another word but has a different meaning or spelling. What are the other homophone pairs you know? Make a list of them.

- Draw a funny picture of a homophone. Write a story about it.

First Word	Second Word
beat	beet
flee	flea
knew	new
male	mail
mane	main
one	won
rode	road
sell	cell
tale	tail
waste	waist

WORD SORT 33:
More Homophones

Sorting Activities

○ Give each student a copy of the word cards (page 61) and Sorting Sheet A (page 27) to sort pairs of homophones. Have students place each pair of homophones side by side on the sorting sheet. (Answers appear at right.)

Spelling Journal

○ A homophone is a word that is pronounced like another word but has a different meaning or spelling. What are the other homophone pairs you know? Make a list of them.

○ Write a funny story about a mix-up involving homophones. Perhaps the characters misunderstood something they heard because they didn't know which homophone was being used.

First Word	Second Word
be	bee
bear	bare
by	buy
for	four
hear	here
hole	whole
meet	meat
see	sea
son	sun
week	weak

WORD SORT 34:
Onomatopoeia

Sorting Activities

○ Give each student a copy of the word cards (page 62) and Sorting Sheet A (page 27) to sort words by noises made by animals vocally and noises made by inanimate objects. (Answers appear at right.)

○ Sort by words that include double letters (repeated letters in a row) and words that do not.

Spelling Journal

○ Onomatopoeia is when words sounds like their meanings or the sounds associated with those words—for example, the word *buzz* sounds like buzzing because of the /z/ sound. What other words can you think of that are onomatopoeic?

Animal Noises	Object Noises
baa	beep
cheep	boom
cuckoo	clang
gobble	clank
meow	click
moo	ding
neigh	splash
quack	thud
tweet	thump
woof	toot

○ Write a "noisy" short story in which everything toots, hisses, or thumps! What objects and animals make these noises? Include words from the list as well ones that aren't on the list.

WORD SORT 35:
Contractions

Sorting Activities

- Give each student a copy of the word cards (page 63) and Sorting Sheet A (page 27) to sort separate words in one column and contractions in the other. Have students line up the separate words with their matching contraction. (Answers appear at right.)

- Sort by words that include pronouns (*I*, *you*, *he*, *she*, and so on) and words that do not.

Spelling Journal

- Write as many other contractions as you can. Then write the two words that form the contraction.

- Write a dialogue that includes lots of contractions. Don't forget to use quotation marks.

Separate Words	Contractions
can not	can't
do not	don't
has not	hasn't
here is	here's
I am	I'm
she will	she'll
they are	they're
we will	we'll
will not	won't
you are	you're

WORD SORT 36:
Compound Words

Sorting Activities

- Give each student a copy of the word cards (page 64) and Sorting Sheet A (page 27). Explain that they should build compound words with the word cards and place them side by side on the sorting sheet. Answers will vary; possible answers appear at right.

Spelling Journal

- Write as many other compound words as you can.

- Write a list poem that includes lots of compound words.

anybody	everybody	playhouse
anyplace	everyplace	playroom
anything	everything	somebody
anywhere	everywhere	someplace
bathhouse	firefly	something
bathroom	firehouse	somewhere
buttercup	firelight	sunbath
butterfly	fireplace	sunlight
campfire	fruitcake	
cupcake	lighthouse	

Note: These do not appear on the Master Word List.

age	blink	cable	chop	cried	elephant
alive	block	cage	chores	crumb	endless
allow	blue	cancel	church	crutch	enough
amuse	boat	candle	circle	cry	excite
apple	boldness	candy	cities	crying	face
ask	boom	can't	claim	cube	fade
asked	booth	captain	clang	cuckoo	families
August	boots	careful	clank	cups	fan
author	both	careless	clap	curve	fast
awake	bounce	carried	clapped	cute	fault
awful	box	carry	claw	dance	feast
baa	boxes	carrying	clean	danced	feed
babies	braid	case	click	dancing	feeling
badge	brave	cash	climb	darkness	feet
bagel	bread	catch	climbed	daughter	fence
bake	breakfast	cattle	cling	dawn	fetch
baked	breeze	caught	clock	deer	field
bare	brick	cause	close	delight	fierce
be	bridge	ceiling	closet	desk	fifteen
beach	brief	cell	cloudy	down	fight
beaches	bringing	center	clown	dime	fish
bear	brisk	chain	club	ding	flag
beat	broken	chance	clue	dishes	flakes
because	brook	change	coaches	ditch	flannel
bee	broom	chase	coal	divide	flaw
beep	brother	chased	coat	don't	flea
beet	brown	chasing	code	down	flee
begging	brush	cheek	cold	dozen	flew
believe	bubble	cheep	comb	draw	flies
bench	bucket	cheerful	cook	drawing	flipping
best	budge	cheese	cooked	drew	float
bike	bunch	chew	corn	drop	floor
bin	buried	chicken	couch	duck	flour
blame	bury	chief	cough	dull	flow
blanket	burying	child	coughed	each	flower
blend	buy	children	count	edge	flute
blew	by	chill	cover	eight	fly
blind	cab	choose	crash	elbow	follow

foot	hardness	judge	loud	nameless	plane
for	hasn't	jump	love	neigh	please
forever	haul	jumped	luck	neighbor	pledge
four	hear	June	lunches	nephew	plow
freeze	hedge	kid	mail	new	plunge
fresh	heel	kindness	main	nickel	pocket
friend	helpful	kite	male	niece	police
friendly	helpless	knee	mane	none	polite
frost	here	knew	mask	noon	pond
frown	here's	knife	match	numb	pools
fudge	high	knight	maze	odd	powder
fuse	hint	knock	meal	of	price
geese	hive	knot	meat	office	prize
globe	hole	know	meet	one	proof
glow	hook	known	menu	organize	punch
glue	hoop	label	meow	orphan	purse
goals	hope	lace	met	other	quack
gobble	hoped	lamb	mice	our	quiz
going	hopeful	lamp	middle	out	race
good	hopeless	large	might	oven	raced
goodness	hoping	last	mile	owl	racing
goose	hopped	late	mine	ox	raft
got	hotel	laugh	mixing	oxen	rage
grab	hour	laughed	moo	page	raid
grabbed	house	laughter	mood	pain	reach
grade	howl	lawn	moose	parcel	reading
grades	huge	lazily	mopping	patted	realize
grand	hugged	learned	mouse	pause	receipt
grapes	human	leave	mouth	paw	receive
graph	hurried	ledge	move	peach	reign
grass	hurry	lend	moved	pebble	reindeer
grease	hurrying	letting	moving	peek	relaxed
great	I'm	life	much	pennies	relief
green	inch	limb	mud	people	rice
grew	inches	limp	mule	person	rich
grief	itch	lock	munch	phone	ridge
grow	jaw	locker	music	photo	rise
growl	jet	look	must	piece	risk
group	joke	loose	nail	pitch	road
happiness	joyful	lose	name	place	roam

rock	sight	stairs	these	try	wise
rode	singing	start	they're	trying	wish
roof	sipping	state	thick	tugging	witch
rope	sitting	steep	thief	tune	woman
rose	size	stirred	thigh	turkey	women
rough	skate	stomp	thing	tweet	won
round	skated	stone	think	unit	won't
rub	skating	stood	thinking	use	woof
rude	ski	stopped	thirty	useful	work
rule	skill	stories	this	useless	worried
running	skillful	stove	those	vain	worry
sad	skin	stretch	though	vein	worrying
sail	skirt	studied	thud	village	worse
scale	sky	study	thumb	vote	would
school	slammed	studying	thump	vowel	wow
scream	sleepless	stuff	tight	wagging	wrap
screen	sleigh	such	time	waist	wrench
sea	sloppy	sun	tipping	wait	wrinkle
see	smell	sunlight	title	walked	wrist
seesaw	smile	table	toast	waste	write
sell	snail	tail	tomatoes	watch	wrong
serve	soak	tale	tonight	weak	wrote
sheep	soap	talking	took	week	yawn
sheet	soft	tapped	tool	weigh	yield
shelf	softness	taste	toot	we'll	you're
she'll	son	tasted	tooth	west	zero
shield	sorted	tasting	tough	whack	zipper
shift	south	taught	towel	whale	
shiny	speaking	tea	town	what	
shirt	spend	teams	trace	wheel	
shoe	spies	tease	track	when	
shook	splash	teeth	trash	where	
shoot	spoke	tell	travel	which	
shopped	sponge	test	treat	while	
should	spoonful	tested	tried	whisper	
shout	spoons	than	tries	white	
shovel	sprinkle	thank	trophy	whole	
shrink	squeeze	that	trot	whose	
sick	stage	their	true	why	
sigh	stain	then	truly	window	

Weekly Word Sorts That Build Spelling Skills · Scholastic Teaching Resources

Name _____ Date _____

Sorting Sheet A

WORD SORT _____

Name _____ Date _____

Sorting Sheet B

WORD SORT _____

Weekly Word Sorts That Build Spelling Skills Scholastic Teaching Resources

WORD SORT 1:

Short *a*, Short *e*, Short *i*

hint	jet	shift
lamp	smell	tell
fresh	grass	sad
wish	lend	this
cab	grand	bin
that	limp	fan
best	met	kid

WORD SORT 2:
Short *o* and Short *u*

pond	love
duck	drop
got	mud
stomp	none
trot	of
dull	sloppy
clock	rub
oven	stuff
lock	odd
jump	box

Weekly Word Sorts That Build Spelling Skills Scholastic Teaching Resources

WORD SORT 3:
Long *a*

claim	nail
maze	face
name	pain
chain	raid
fade	sail
braid	brave
plane	late
rage	snail
wait	vain
scale	bake

Weekly Word Sorts That Build Spelling Skills Scholastic Teaching Resources

feast	feed	peek
yield	tea	scream
leave	cheek	squeeze
shield	screen	grief
meal	brief	peach
niece	heel	steep
grease	chief	piece

Weekly Word Sorts That Build Spelling Skills Scholastic Teaching Resources

WORD SORT 5:
Long *i*

alive	sight
might	tight
mine	divide
tonight	high
bike	polite
sunlight	thigh
sigh	time
dime	delight
hive	wise
mile	fight

Weekly Word Sorts That Build Spelling Skills Scholastic Teaching Resources

WORD SORT 6:

Long _o_

stove	globe	window
follow	coal	toast
vote	roam	spoke
glow	float	elbow
boat	known	soak
code	rope	flow
grow	soap	joke

WORD SORT 7:

/o͝o/ and /o͞o/

good	school
mood	brook
noon	broom
hook	cook
look	stood
moose	would
roof	shoot
shook	tool
should	boots
took	hoop

chew	rule
menu	music
drew	fuse
glue	blue
cube	mule
June	amuse
rude	tune
human	cute
use	booth
clue	unit

loud	owl
down	cloudy
growl	frown
south	plow
howl	hour
out	powder
mouth	town
round	count
allow	our
bounce	wow

WORD SORT 10:
au and *aw*

seesaw	draw
August	pause
fault	lawn
yawn	taught
author	claw
cause	flaw
haul	because
dawn	paw
awful	caught
daughter	jaw

Weekly Word Sorts That Build Spelling Skills Scholastic Teaching Resources

eight	receipt
believe	friendly
chief	niece
reindeer	relief
piece	ceiling
vein	thief
field	receive
weigh	neighbor
sleigh	fierce
friend	reign

Blends *br*, *gr*, *tr*

true	breeze	grew
bread	group	travel
truly	brick	grade
great	green	brother
breakfast	trace	treat
broken	brown	grapes
grab	track	tries

blind	clean	clown
close	blame	flag
blanket	cling	blend
flute	blink	flower
fly	flew	blew
block	closet	club
clap	floor	flour

WORD SORT 14:
Initial and Ending Blends *sk* and *st*

ski	west
fast	mask
sky	skirt
last	desk
stairs	skill
start	risk
test	state
stain	brisk
ask	stone
skin	must

Weekly Word Sorts That Build Spelling Skills Scholastic Teaching Resources

church	brush
shoe	shout
couch	chill
shirt	cash
reach	crash
chance	chop
beach	trash
cheese	sheet
bunch	fish
chores	shiny

what	then
thing	whale
wheel	both
thirty	white
when	why
think	other
though	where
whisper	thick
their	while
whack	than

bench	such
pitch	which
stretch	each
much	watch
punch	witch
reach	inch
ditch	catch
munch	crutch
fetch	itch
rich	match

WORD SORT 18:
Words With /f/

elephant	cough	rough
tough	enough	life
photo	orphan	graph
shelf	coughed	proof
spoonful	fifteen	nephew
trophy	forever	raft
laugh	laughter	phone

Weekly Word Sorts That Build Spelling Skills   Scholastic Teaching Resources

WORD SORT 19:
Words With /k/

candy	awake	captain
chicken	baked	turkey
corn	shrink	work
luck	rock	locker
cover	sick	cold
pocket	thank	coat
curve	kite	bucket

WORD SORT 20:

Words With /z/

zero	prize
lose	these
lazily	quiz
organize	those
rise	whose
realize	zipper
please	choose
rose	cheese
freeze	dozen
tease	size

Weekly Word Sorts That Build Spelling Skills Scholastic Teaching Resources

knee	wrote	wrist
crumb	lamb	knock
wrench	knife	climb
thumb	know	knot
knew	write	limb
wrinkle	numb	wrap
comb	knight	wrong

dge and *ge*

badge	plunge
stage	ledge
large	ridge
edge	age
sponge	judge
fudge	pledge
bridge	cage
village	change
budge	huge
page	hedge

c and s

center	rice
spend	lace
worse	case
circle	place
serve	frost
office	house
loose	excite
police	soft
purse	fence
price	smile

Weekly Word Sorts That Build Spelling Skills   Scholastic Teaching Resources

WORD SORT 24:
Plurals

cups	grades	teams
lunches	dishes	babies
flakes	pools	boxes
inches	stories	cities
tomatoes	spoons	families
goals	spies	pennies
beaches	flies	coaches

Weekly Word Sorts That Build Spelling Skills Scholastic Teaching Resources

WORD SORT 25:
Unusual Plurals

people	feet
child	person
deer	sheep
teeth	mice
foot	tooth
women	children
goose	oxen
mouse	woman
deer	geese
ox	sheep

Weekly Word Sorts That Build Spelling Skills Scholastic Teaching Resources

apple	middle
label	pebble
nickel	parcel
bubble	shovel
candle	sprinkle
towel	flannel
cable	table
vowel	bagel
cattle	title
hotel	cancel

WORD SORT 27:
-ed Verbs

asked	jumped
patted	laughed
shopped	grabbed
learned	clapped
hopped	slammed
hugged	climbed
sorted	cooked
tested	stirred
walked	relaxed
tapped	stopped

WORD SORT 28:
-ing Verbs

sitting	speaking
going	running
sipping	talking
feeling	thinking
mixing	begging
letting	flipping
reading	mopping
tugging	bringing
wagging	drawing
singing	tipping

Weekly Word Sorts That Build Spelling Skills Scholastic Teaching Resources

dance	moved	skating
race	dancing	tasted
danced	move	chasing
moving	taste	hoping
chased	racing	chase
hope	raced	skate
hoped	skated	tasting

WORD SORT 30:
y to *i* Verbs

bury	trying	carrying
hurrying	worry	hurried
try	cry	tried
studying	carried	worried
hurry	cried	crying
buried	carry	studied
study	burying	worrying

Weekly Word Sorts That Build Spelling Skills Scholastic Teaching Resources

careful	boldness	cheerful
darkness	careless	useful
hopeless	hopeful	happiness
joyful	endless	sleepless
softness	kindness	helpful
helpless	nameless	hardness
skillful	goodness	useless

WORD SORT 32:
Homophones

rode	flea
flee	main
male	new
tail	beat
knew	mane
one	road
tale	won
sell	mail
waste	cell
beet	waist

Weekly Word Sorts That Build Spelling Skills Scholastic Teaching Resources

WORD SORT 33:

More Homophones

be	four
see	by
for	bee
meet	buy
sun	here
bear	whole
hole	weak
hear	bare
son	sea
week	meat

WORD SORT 34:
Onomatopoeia

baa	thud
gobble	moo
toot	clang
boom	woof
click	clank
quack	ding
cheep	cuckoo
beep	meow
tweet	thump
neigh	splash

Weekly Word Sorts That Build Spelling Skills Scholastic Teaching Resources

Contractions

won't	can not
has not	we'll
don't	will not
she will	here is
can't	hasn't
they are	do not
we will	I'm
they're	she'll
you are	I am
here's	you're

Compound Words

any	fruit
bath	house
body	light
butter	place
cake	play
camp	room
cup	some
every	sun
fire	thing
fly	where

Weekly Word Sorts That Build Spelling Skills Scholastic Teaching Resources